# Funny & Fabulous
# Story Prompts

## 50 Reproducible Story Starters
## To Get Them Writing
## and Loving It!

### By Richie Chevat

NEW YORK • TORONTO • LONDON • AUCKLAND • SYDNEY
MEXICO CITY • NEW DELHI • HONG KONG

Cover design by Jaime Lucero
Cover illustration by Valeria Petrone
Interior design by LDL Designs
Interior illustration by Stephen Lewis

ISBN 0-590-96732-0

Copyright © 1998 by Richie Chevat

# Table of Contents

Dear Teachers,

As someone who writes for a living, I can testify that there is nothing as frightening as a blank page. Worrying about how to start can be the surest way to a bad case of writer's block, whether you're beginning your tenth novel or writing your first story ever.

Since professional writers often need creative jump starts, I thought new writers could use some, too. That's where *Funny & Fabulous Story Prompts* comes in. Each reproducible page offers the beginning of a story—just two or three sentences to spark young writers' imaginations and get their pencils moving. *Beginning* is the key word here. I've tried to design the opening lines to allow kids great freedom in deciding what happens next, which means each tale written in your class will be absolutely original, absolutely unique.

Nurturing the creative impulse is the first and most important step in learning how to transform thoughts into written words. I hope these story prompts will help your students unlock the doors to their imaginations and establish a lifelong love of writing.

—Richie Chevat

# How to Use This Book

Welcome to *Funny & Fabulous Story Prompts*! This book is designed to spark the imagination of every writer in your class. The story starters are divided into eight separate books, each containing a cover sheet and six or seven story ideas. I've chosen topics that I know from experience will appeal to young learners—fantasy, science fiction, animals, spooky stories, fractured fairy tales, and more.

Before kids start writing, make sure they understand that there is no right or wrong way to complete the stories. Whichever narrative path their tales take, the important thing is for children to express themselves freely, practice and polish their writing, and stretch their imaginations.

As children work on their stories, encourage them to consider the various elements that go into making a story interesting for the reader: plot, character, setting, plenty of details, and some good old-fashioned action. The story prompts in this book will certainly lead young writers in the right direction!

These starters also present great opportunities for students to practice the writing process. As children think through their stories, they can use blank sheets of paper to write their drafts and revise. Once they're happy with the tale, they can write the final draft on the reproducible page (using the blank line template on page 64 if they need more room).

There's no prescribed method for using these story starters. Some students may like a variety, writing stories from different sections of the book; others may choose to finish some or all of the stories in a section and compile them, with the cover page, into an eye-catching chapter book. All they need to do next is add a page about the author to the back of their books, then they're ready to share published writing with classmates, friends, and family.

# The Strangest Day

By

_____

## Story 1
# A Weird Wake-up

Today was the strangest day of my whole life. When I woke up, it was raining inside my room! I went to the bathroom to brush my teeth and the toothpaste was black instead of white! Everything was the opposite. First, I put on my shoes. Then, I pulled my socks on over them, and...

_____

_____

_____

_____

_____

_____

_____

_____

_____

_____

_____

_____

# Story 2: Even Robots Need Breakfast

This morning, a robot was in my kitchen!

"What are you doing here?" I asked.

"Making a cheeseburger," he answered.

"A cheeseburger?" I asked. "That's not a proper breakfast. Why don't you make _____?"
                                                          breakfast food

The robot beeped. His metal head spun around, and then…

_____

_____

_____

_____

_____

_____

_____

_____

_____

_____

_____

Scholastic Professional Books • Funny & Fabulous Story Prompts

### Story 3
# Monkey See, Monkey Do

Today, on the way to school, I saw a pack of wild monkeys! I waved. They waved back. I stuck out my tongue. They stuck out their tongues. I started to run. They started to run, too. Then I...

_____

_____

_____

_____

_____

_____

_____

_____

_____

_____

_____

## Story 4
# A BIG Day at School

When I got to school today, there was a giant standing at the front door. He was about 100 feet tall. Each of his feet was as big as a school bus.

"I am a new boy at school," he said. "This is my first day."

I couldn't believe it! I asked him...

_____

_____

_____

_____

_____

_____

_____

_____

_____

_____

_____

_____

## Story 5
# The Recess Mess

Today during recess, a large truck pulled up to the school yard.

"Someone ordered 100 _____ ," the truck driver said. "We are
_kind of toy_

also delivering 10,000 pounds of _____ and 50,000 gallons of
_type of food_

_____ ."
_type of drink_

The truck driver backed the truck onto the soccer field and...

_____

_____

_____

_____

_____

_____

_____

_____

_____

_____

_____

_____

_____

## Story 6
# A Crazy Class

Today all the pictures we drew in art class came to life. I drew an airplane and it flew around the room. Then I drew a _____ and it...

_____

_____

_____

_____

_____

_____

_____

_____

_____

_____

_____

Scholastic Professional Books • Funny & Fabulous Story Prompts

## Story 7
# Aliens Ate My Homework

Today, as I was walking home from school, a spaceship landed right in front of me! An alien with eyes like a cat and long spidery legs came out.

"I am hungry," he said. "I have come to your planet in search of books to eat."

"Books aren't food," I said.

"That's the craziest thing I ever heard," said the alien. "I love a good book! Right now I am craving a big fat math book."

He started to walk towards me and…

_____

_____

_____

_____

_____

_____

_____

_____

_____

_____

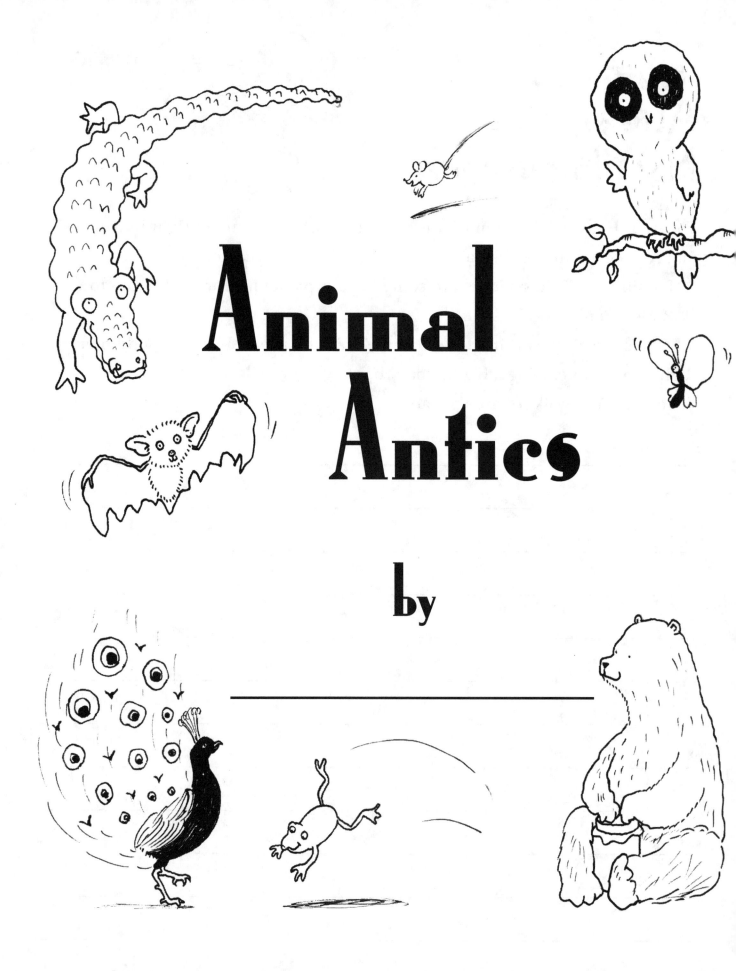

# Animal Antics

## by

_____

Scholastic Professional Books • Funny & Fabulous Story Prompts

# Story 1:
# Curious Critters

Ollie the Owl was always asking questions. "Who are you?" he would ask. "Who, who?" His best friend Willy Wolf also had a lot of questions. "How old are you? Howl, howl!" Together, they went on a trip through the woods. You'll never guess who they ran into next. It was …

_____

_____

_____

_____

_____

_____

_____

_____

_____

_____

_____

_____

_____

# Story 2: Big Mouse

Alexander the Mouse was proud. He had a long name. And he had such a big shadow, he could even scare an elephant!

Ellie the Elephant had just received a large hunk of cheese as a birthday gift, and Alexander really wanted it, so he came up with a plan....

_____

_____

_____

_____

_____

_____

_____

_____

_____

_____

_____

_____

# Story 3: The Bear's Dream

One autumn, a large brown bear named
Growly curled up in his cave for his long
winter's sleep. Soon he started to dream. In
his dream he could eat all the honey he
wanted and…

_____

_____

_____

_____

_____

_____

_____

_____

_____

_____

_____

_____

# Story 4: 'Gator Aid

Frannie the Frog was tired and she needed to cross a stream to get home. A big old alligator named Tex offered her a ride on his back.

"You'll try to eat me," said Frannie.

"I promise I won't eat you if you'll teach me how to make those cool croaking sounds," said Tex.

So Frannie hopped onto his back and then…

_____

_____

_____

_____

_____

_____

_____

_____

_____

_____

_____

# Story 5: Forest Fight

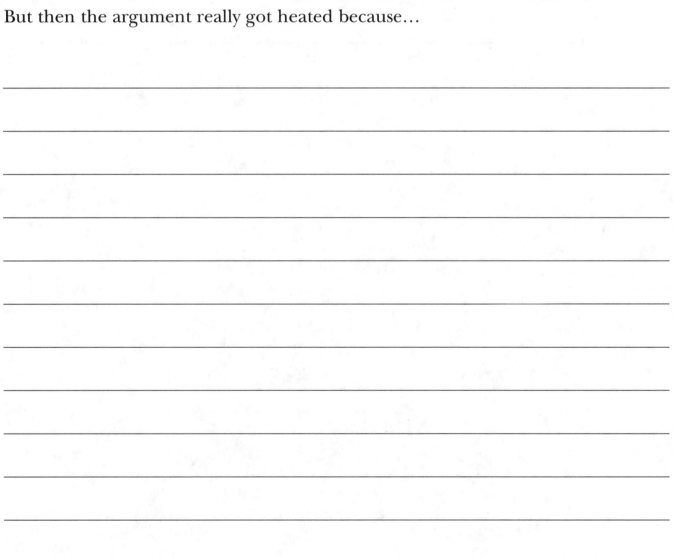

One of the biggest arguments in the history of the forest happened between Madam Butterfly and Pierre the Peacock.

"I am the most beautiful animal," said Madam. "Look at my colors, gaze at my stripes!"

"You're just a bug," said Pierre. "You're not even one of the animals."

"At least I can fly," said Madam. "Walking bird, walking bird, ha,ha,ha!" But then the argument really got heated because…

_____

_____

_____

_____

_____

_____

_____

_____

_____

_____

# Story 6: Gone Batty

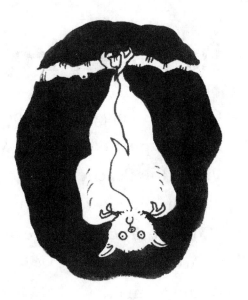

Bart the Bat got sick and tired of hanging upside down. He didn't like living in a cave. He didn't like eating flies. He didn't like sleeping during the day. Now bunnies, *they* had all the fun. So Bart the Bat decided to become Bart the Bunny. Here is what happened…

_____

_____

_____

_____

_____

_____

_____

_____

_____

_____

_____

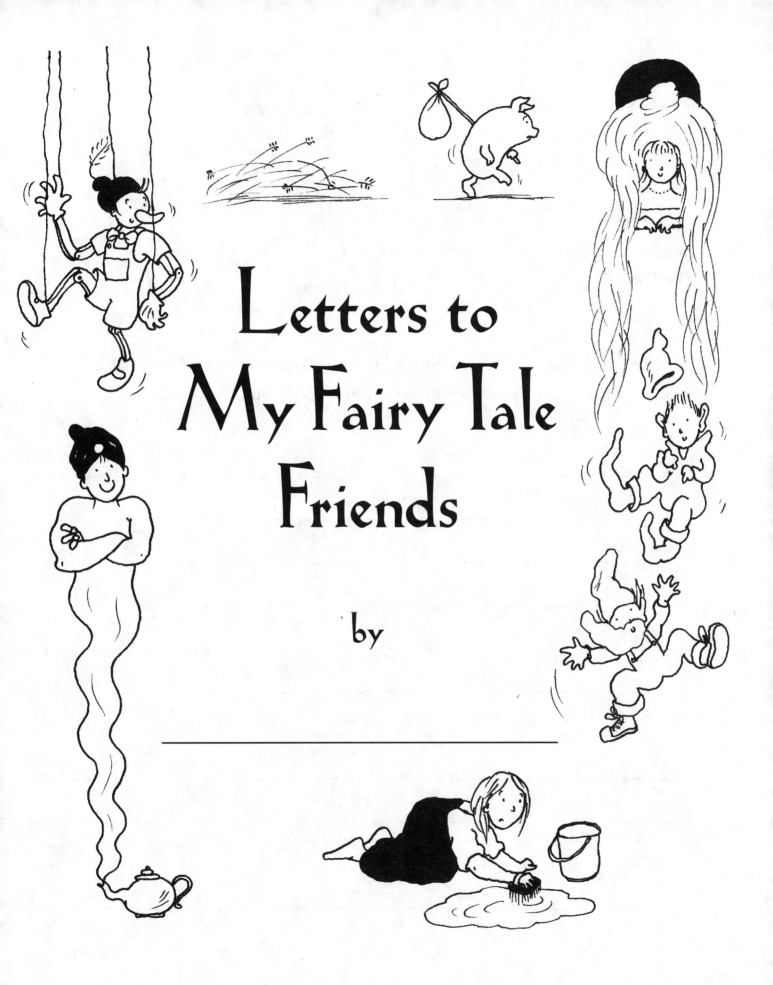

# Letters to My Fairy Tale Friends

by

_____

# Letter 1
# Date _____

**Snow White**
**Dwarves Cottage**
**The Forest**

Dear Snow White,

Say hello to the seven dwarves for me. Tell old Grumpy to cheer up. I also wanted to warn you about the Queen. I think you should…

_____

_____

_____

_____

_____

_____

_____

_____

_____

_____

Scholastic Professional Books • *Funny & Fabulous Story Prompts*

# Letter 2
## Date _____

**Cinderella**
**Evil Stepmother's House**
**22 Pumpkin Lane**

Dear Cinderella,

I am sorry everyone's so mean to you. It's not fair. You do so much work, you should get to have a good time. I think I know how you can have more fun. You should…

_____

_____

_____

_____

_____

_____

_____

_____

_____

# Letter 3

Date _____

**Magic Genie**
**The Lamp**
**Aladdin's Palace**

Dear Genie,

How do you fit in that lamp? I know you must get a lot of letters. I hope you have time to answer this one. I heard you can grant three wishes. My wishes are…

_____

_____

_____

_____

_____

_____

_____

_____

_____

_____

Scholastic Professional Books • Funny & Fabulous Story Prompts

# Letter 4

Date _____

**First Little Pig**
**Straw House**
**Wolf Road**

Dear First Little Pig,

I understand that you live in a house made of straw. Be careful! I think you may get a visit from the Big Bad Wolf.  If he comes, I think you should play a big trick on him. Here's an idea....

_____

_____

_____

_____

_____

_____

_____

_____

_____

# Letter 5
## Date _____

**Rapunzel**
**Tallest Craggy Tower**
**Cold Stone Castle**

Dear Rapunzel,

I was sorry to hear you got locked in the tower. Boy, that sounds awful! No one to talk to! No shampoo! I am writing to say it is time for you to take matters into your own hands and escape. Here's one way to do it....

_____

_____

_____

_____

_____

_____

_____

_____

_____

Scholastic Professional Books • Funny & Fabulous Story Prompts

# Letter 6

**Date** _____

**Pinnochio**
**Gepetto's Workshop**
**154 Woodcut Drive**

Dear Pinnochio,

I heard you are made of wood. Is that really true?

I also heard you want to become a real boy. But

I think it would be better for you to become a real

_____ because. . .
type of animal

_____

_____

_____

_____

_____

_____

_____

_____

_____

# Real-Life
# Adventures

## by

---

# Story #1
# Surprise in Store

One day, as Joe was sweeping up his parents' grocery store, he saw something strange on one of the shelves. It was _____.
Next thing you know, …

_____

_____

_____

_____

_____

_____

_____

_____

_____

_____

_____

_____

_____

# Story #2
# What a Hit!

Ellen was the right fielder on her base-
ball team. A batter hit a long home run
that rolled into the bushes. Ellen ran after it.
She was looking around trying to find the ball when all of a sudden…

_____

_____

_____

_____

_____

_____

_____

_____

_____

_____

_____

_____

# Story #3
# The New Kid

Jessie was the new kid in school. Every day at lunch time she sat by herself. She missed all her old friends. But one day a girl named Tabitha sat down beside her. Jessie and Tabitha became friends right away because…

_____

_____

_____

_____

_____

_____

_____

_____

_____

_____

_____

_____

# Story #4
# Paul's Play

Paul was very excited about the class play.
He had the best part. He got to play a
_____ . But while
type of character
performing in front of the whole school,
he was shocked when...

_____

_____

_____

_____

_____

_____

_____

_____

_____

_____

_____

_____

Scholastic Professional Books • Funny & Fabulous Story Prompts

# Story #5
# A Trip Downtown

On Saturday, Lisa's mother took her shopping.
They went into a very big store. Lisa saw a
_____ . She asked her mother
type of item
if she could have it, and then …

_____

_____

_____

_____

_____

_____

_____

_____

_____

_____

_____

_____

# Story #6
# A Birthday Wish

Steven was having a great birthday party!  It was time for the cake. His mom brought it out. The cake was covered with green and yellow icing. Steve took a deep breath, blew out the candles, and wished for…

_____

_____

_____

_____

_____

_____

_____

_____

_____

_____

_____

_____

Scholastic Professional Books • Funny & Fabulous Story Prompts

# Report to Planet Zog

## by Zeekrog

(_____)

# Report #1
To: General Zokrog, Planet Zog
From: Zeekrog the Spy

# About School

Dear General Zokrog,

As you know, on Planet Zog we are born knowing everything. But here on Earth humans have to learn at a place called school. I will attempt to tell you about school. It is…

_____

_____

_____

_____

_____

_____

_____

_____

_____

_____

_____

**Report #2**
**To: General Zokrog, Planet Zog**
**From: Zeekrog the Spy**

# About Food

Dear General Zokrog,

On Planet Zog we eat only tomatoes and light bulbs.
We eat through our ears, of course. But humans
have very different eating habits. What do people
eat? How do they eat it? I will explain. First of all, …

_____

_____

_____

_____

_____

_____

_____

_____

_____

_____

_____

_____

# Report #3
## To: General Zokrog, Planet Zog
## From: Zeekrog the Spy
# About Houses

Dear General Zokrog,

As you know, on Planet Zog we all live in giant blue radishes. But here on Earth, humans live in something called a house. Houses are strange places. Let me tell you about them...

_____

_____

_____

_____

_____

_____

_____

_____

_____

Scholastic Professional Books • Funny & Fabulous Story Prompts

# Report #4
## To: General Zokrog, Planet Zog
## From: Zeekrog the Spy
# About Friends

Dear General Zokrog,

Humans have something we do not have on
Planet Zog. They call them "friends." Friends
are very important to humans. Let me tell you about friends...

_____

_____

_____

_____

_____

_____

_____

_____

_____

_____

# Report #5
## To: General Zokrog, Planet Zog
## From: Zeekrog the Spy
# About Games

Dear General Zokrog,

On Planet Zog we love to play a game where we point at the sky and yell "Iko Iko Iko!" Children on Zog like to pretend they are termites. These humans have very strange games. I will try to tell you about a human game. It is called _____ . This is how you play…
type of game

_____

_____

_____

_____

_____

_____

_____

_____

# Report #6
## To: General Zokrog, Planet Zog
## From: Zeekrog the Spy
# About Weather

Dear General Zokrog,

On Planet Zog raindrops are as big as your head. Clouds are yellow and shaped like ducks, of course. Weather on Earth is very strange. Some of the things that happen include…

_____

_____

_____

_____

_____

_____

_____

_____

_____

_____

# Spooky
# Stories
by

_____

Scholastic Professional Books • Funny & Fabulous Story Prompts

# Story 1
# Scary School

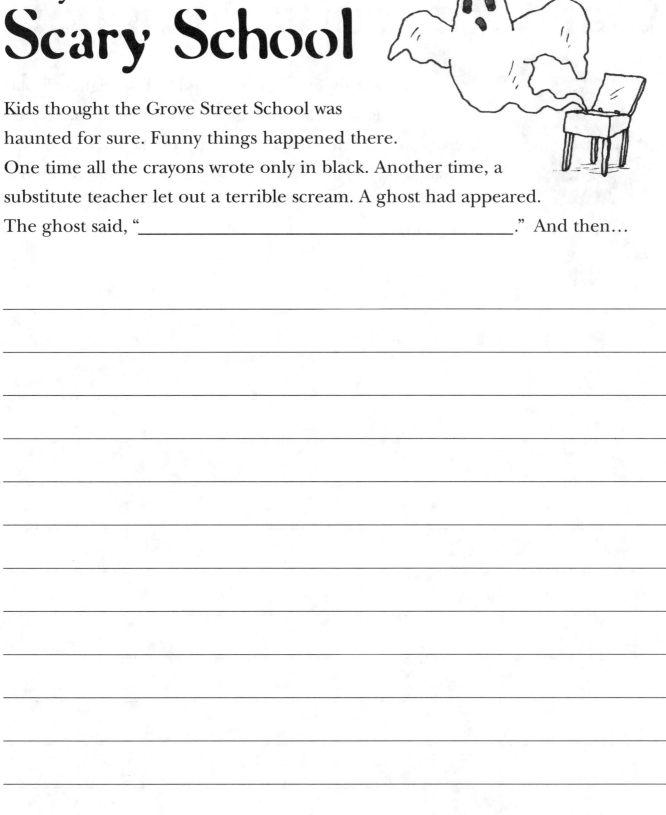

Kids thought the Grove Street School was
haunted for sure. Funny things happened there.
One time all the crayons wrote only in black. Another time, a
substitute teacher let out a terrible scream. A ghost had appeared.
The ghost said, "_____." And then…

_____

_____

_____

_____

_____

_____

_____

_____

_____

_____

## Story 2
# Cat Got Your Tongue?

Sam was always a little spooked by his neighbor's black cat, Midnight. Midnight was always slinking around, as if she were spying. Then one day, Midnight blinked her yellow eyes and said, "Hello Sam." Sam was so scared he couldn't even say anything in reply. Then, Midnight said something that really shocked him…

_____

_____

_____

_____

_____

_____

_____

_____

_____

_____

_____

_____

_____

Scholastic Professional Books • Funny & Fabulous Story Prompts

# Trick or T-Rex?

On Halloween, Alice was a witch. Her best friend Emily was a dinosaur. They went from house to house Trick or Treating.

"Hey," said Alice. "Let's count up how much candy we have."

"Grrrrrl," said Emily.

"Stop being silly," said Alice.

"Grrrrl," said Emily again.

Alice reached to peel off Emily's dinosaur mask and that was when she saw that…

_____

_____

_____

_____

_____

_____

_____

_____

_____

# Ha, Ha, Very Mummy

Gary and his friend Will were at the museum on a class field trip. While the class went ahead, they stopped to look at a mummy on display.

"Look at that mummy!" Gary said. "I wonder who he was."

"I'd show you, but I'm all wrapped up right now," the mummy replied.

Gary and Will jumped in fright. And then...

_____

_____

_____

_____

_____

_____

_____

_____

_____

_____

_____

_____

_____

# Little Pet Shop of Horrors

Pete's Pet Shop was a creepy place. It didn't have
any kittens or puppies. Instead, it specialized in
snakes and bats. Mary Anne needed to buy
food for her parrot, Polly. Slowly she walked
past the cages. Then she stopped. She couldn't
believe it! In one of the cages was a...

_____

_____

_____

_____

_____

_____

_____

_____

_____

_____

# Story 6
# It Came from the TV

Tim loved to watch a TV show called *Don't You Dare Watch This Scary Show*. He didn't think it was scary at all. But one afternoon, when he turned on the TV, something scary did happen. As soon as the show came on…

_____

_____

_____

_____

_____

_____

_____

_____

_____

_____

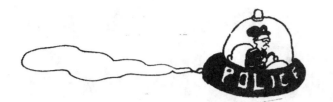

# What Will Happen in the Future?

### by

_____

## Story 1
# Jobs of Tomorrow

What types of work will people do in the future?
Will we need police officers in outer space, or
underwater home builders? Here are some of the
jobs I think people will have....

_____

_____

_____

_____

_____

_____

_____

_____

_____

_____

_____

_____

## Story 2

# Travel in the Future

Today, people travel in cars, trains or planes. In the future it will be very different. Maybe you'll ride everywhere in a space car. Or maybe there will be special time travel machines. In the future, people might even travel by…

_____

_____

_____

_____

_____

_____

_____

_____

_____

_____

_____

_____

## Story 3
# Space-Age Schools

Even in the future, children will still have to learn. Will kids be taught by special talking computers? Will there still be schools or will kids learn at home? Here is what I think will happen…

_____

_____

_____

_____

_____

_____

_____

_____

_____

_____

_____

# Story 4
# Future Fun

In today's world, playing games, listening to
music, watching television, and going on trips
are just some of the ways people have fun. What will people in the future do for
fun?  Maybe there will be new types of super realistic video games. Perhaps someone will invent a brand new sport.  In the future, to have fun, I think people will…

_____

_____

_____

_____

_____

_____

_____

_____

_____

_____

_____

_____

# Story 5
# Life in Space

In the future, people may live in outer space. Maybe there will be cities on the Moon. When people go on trips maybe they will stay in space hotels. What will it be like to live in space? I think people will...

_____

_____

_____

_____

_____

_____

_____

_____

_____

_____

_____

_____

**Story 6**

# 100 Years From Now

The world is very different now from 100 years ago. What will it be like 100 years in the future? Will the world be a better place or worse? Will some people move to the moon? Or live in homes under the sea? Will America have 100 states instead of 50? It's hard to know. But I think the world in the future will be…

_____

_____

_____

_____

_____

_____

_____

_____

_____

# Super Monkey

## by

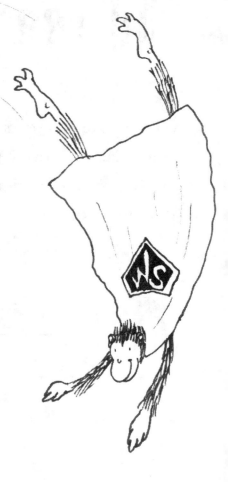

_____

# Story #1
# A Bunch of Bad Guys

"Help!" yelled Mr. Carter, president of the First
Banana Bank. "I've been robbed!"

Someone had stolen all of the bank's
bananas! Who would catch the crooks? Just
then Mr. Carter spotted something flying
through the sky.

"Is it a bird?" he asked. "Is it a plane?"

No, it was Super Monkey! Super Monkey
flew down to the bank. Then he…

_____

_____

_____

_____

_____

_____

_____

_____

_____

_____

# Story #2
# Boy Super Monkey

Super Monkey wasn't always super. When he was born at the Chimp City Hospital, his mother and father were very happy. They named him Norman. Norman was just a regular baby monkey. Then one day he…

_____

_____

_____

_____

_____

_____

_____

_____

_____

_____

_____

# Story #3
# Cold-Hearted Criminal

It was the first day of spring. Evil Emperor
Penguin, Super Monkey's arch enemy, had
invented a special machine that turned a
nice day into a cold winter day. He was pointing the machine at Chimp City.

"Help!" everyone cried. "We need Super Monkey!"

In a flash, Super Monkey was there. The first thing he did was...

_____

_____

_____

_____

_____

_____

_____

_____

_____

_____

# Story #4
# Who Took the Monkey Lisa?

Someone had stolen *The Monkey Lisa,* the most famous painting in the world.

Mike Monk, head of the Chimp City Museum, shouted, "We need Super Monkey!"

Super Monkey appeared in a flash.

"Don't worry!" he told everyone. "Super Monkey is here!" Then he…

_____

_____

_____

_____

_____

_____

_____

_____

_____

_____

# Story #5
# Space Apes

One day a large spaceship landed
in Chimp City. It was shaped like a
banana! Out walked little green apes!
Everyone ran in fear.

"Apes from space!" they cried. "Help! Help us!"

Far away, Super Monkey heard them with his powerful Super Monkey ears.
He zoomed to the city and…

_____

_____

_____

_____

_____

_____

_____

_____

_____

_____

_____

# Story #6
# Driven Bananas

Super Monkey was flying high above Chimp City
when he heard a loud screeching sound like a car
peeling out. Using his Super Monkey radar vision,
he saw that someone had stolen his Banana Mobile.
The thief was headed right for the Chimp City Hall.
So Super Monkey…

_____

_____

_____

_____

_____

_____

_____

_____

_____

_____

_____

# Story #7
# Super Monkey Day

It was Super Monkey Day. The good citizens of Chimp City wanted to thank Super Monkey for all his help. Mayor Bob Boone delivered a speech. They held a parade with banana-shaped floats. But halfway through the parade, Super Monkey noticed that trouble was brewing. What happened then was …

_____

_____

_____

_____

_____

_____

_____

_____

_____

_____

_____

Scholastic Professional Books • Funny & Fabulous Story Prompts